A GARDEN STYLE BOOK

CACTUS & SUCCULENTS

[SIMPLE SECRETS FOR GLORIOUS GARDENS—INDOORS AND OUT]

MIMI LUEBBERMANN
PHOTOGRAPHY BY FAITH ECHTERMEYER

CHRONICLE BOOKS
SAN FRANCISCO

Text copyright © 1997 by Mimi Luebbermann.
Photographs copyright © 1997 by Faith Echtermeyer.

Library of Congress Cataloging-in-Publication Data:
Luebbermann, Mimi.
Cactus & succulents: simple secrets for glorious
gardens—indoors and out/by Mimi Luebbermann;
photography by Faith Echtermeyer.
       p.   cm.
"A Garden Style Book."
Includes bibliographical references and index.
ISBN 0-8118-1446-7 (pbk.)
1. Cactus. 2. Succulents. 3. Container gardening.
I. Title.
SB438.L84 1997
635.9'3347—dc20   96-28041
                    CIP

Printed in Hong Kong

Cover and interior design by
Aufuldish & Warinner

Distributed in Canada by Raincoast Books,
8680 Cambie Street, Vancouver, B.C. V6P 6M9

10 9 8 7 6 5 4 3 2 1

Chronicle Books
85 Second Street
San Francisco, CA 94105

Web Site: www.chronbooks.com

DEDICATION

From Mimi to Ruth Bancroft, who created
and has for many years maintained the Ruth
Bancroft Garden in Walnut Creek, California,
with a splendid sensitivity to the diversity of
textures and colors of cactus and succulents
resulting in a garden that is a tapestry of the
pleasure from the beauty of her plantings.

Also to Susan and Tony Luebbermann, who
first shared with me their Arizona desert, its
plant and animals, and who understand and
appreciate its true magnificence.

Contents

A WINDOWSILL GARDEN   42

INDOOR POTTED GARDENS   56

INTRODUCTION

Gardeners unexpectedly fall in love with cacti and succulents, and why not? Tiny plants explode with brilliant flowers. Large cacti exotically unfold water-lily-like blooms to softly perfume the night air. With geometric regularity, cacti spines march in swirls or lines or hide behind coats of white hairlike fleece. The cool-toned leaves of succulents are formed like minimalist sculptures, each plant displaying intriguing shapes and blossoms.

¶The neophyte quickly discovers the joys of growing plants that prefer minimal care, perform stoically in arid areas, mix attractively with perennials in garden beds, and show off handsomely in containers, indoors and out. A little neglect doesn't deter the plants from growing, blooming, or multiplying, forming new plants continually from the old. Besides, these plants surprise. Some climb trees, and others grow as large as trees. Hardy species survive winter drifts of snow, and many species can be propagated from just a leaf.

A Cautionary Note
Cactus rustlers and succulent burglars actively denude deserts and forests of desirable cactus and succulent plants, ripping out even 30-foot-high saguaros. Many types of cacti and succulents have become extinct in the wild and are rare in private collections. Make sure that you buy plants from reputable nurseries and, in case of rare types, that the suppliers are selling stock they have propagated or grown from seed.

¶Cacti are native to the Americas, but they have been naturalized in many other regions of the world. Succulents grow all over the world. Long have these plants been used to humankind. The Aztecs wove the fibers of a succulent, the century plant, Agave americana, into a durable cloth. The thorns of many different cactus species were used by early inhabitants of Peru as knitting needles. (As a side note on contemporary use, during the era of the gramophone, the needles transmitting the scratchy sounds were cactus spines.) The hallucinogenic buttons of Lophophora williamsii, known as peyote, have had a place in sacred Native American ceremonies for centuries. The sap of an Agave tequilana is fermented to make tequila.

¶The desert of the American Southwest yields little usable wood. Early builders turned to the large saguaro, Carnegiea gigantea, using the ribs as a material in houses and corrals. Cacti and some succulents, carefully planted and pruned, are still used throughout the world as impenetrable living fences to contain livestock and protect them from predators.

¶In locations in North and South America with so little rainfall that most crops fail, Opuntia have long been used for their edible flat pads and fruit. Imported to arid parts of the globe, these cacti have been incorporated into many contemporary cuisines, including North African, Indian, Middle Eastern, Australian, and South American. The pads, peeled and diced or sliced, taste a bit like cucumber in stews or fresh salsa. Dried, they can be steeped for tea. Jewel-colored cactus fruits called tunas, some deliciously scented like strawberries, are eaten out of hand or stewed into preserves. Although diners may find the seeds too plentiful, Native Americans ground them for flour. Contemporary American chefs have discovered that the ground seeds produce a powder that tastes like an exotic spice, combining the flavors of cinnamon, chocolate, and cumin.

¶Christopher Columbus stumbled across Melocactus on an island in the West Indies. Until he returned home with a collection of cacti, Europeans had never seen them before. First imported to Europe in the eighteenth and nineteenth centuries, cacti and succulents never suffered from the flurry of excitement and high prices orchids and bulbs inspired. Europeans marveled at their many splendors, and amateur gardeners found that the ease of cultivation of most species made them successful plants in the home or greenhouse, although then, as now, many died from

overwatering. In the United States, cacti drew the attention of plant genius Luther Burbank, who experimented with the hybridization of cactus and, eventually, produced a variety of spineless Opuntia still available in nurseries.

¶I had my first cactus experience as a child growing up in Florida when I witnessed the outrageous, one-night-only blossoms of what I think must have been the night-blooming Selenicereus grandiflorus, a climbing cactus with the common name of queen-of-the-night. Our plant skinnied up a cabbage palm outside our back door. My father, who was not an enthusiastic gardener, waited year-round for its bloom, watching with ever-growing anticipation the buds grow fatter and fatter day by day. As the first night arrived, I remember dashing out excitedly after dinner to view the blooms' opening. Every year, we counted the totals. The record was sixteen blooms in a night. The next day, I fancied the spent blooms looked like flamingo heads, pink and naked after the delicate display of the night before.

¶Years later, my mother, then a widow, moved to Tucson, Arizona, and I learned more about cactus. My brother and sister-in-law, who love the desert, shared with me the lore of the stately saguaro and its springtime inhabitant, the cactus wren, nesting safely and contentedly in its hollows. As a mother with young children, I experienced the prickly truth of cactus, as my elder child, chasing a horny toad, fell into the clutches of a nearby spiny onlooker. Tweezers and sticky tape were put to work to extricate the thorns from the tender skin of the stricken toad hunter.

¶Living in mild-winter California, I learned about succulents as an all-purpose garden plant that brought symmetry and a special palette of colors to my garden. Although I am a gardener who likes the soft, blowsy nature of roses, salvias, and luxuriant shrubs, I have come to appreciate succulents and cacti for their hardiness, their tailored beauty, and their generous nature, which allows a new plant to be started by rooting a twig, side shoot, or with some types even a leaf. They make superb pot plants, living in containers with little care or attention, but perform as if you were feeding them miracle food. For gardeners discouraged by failures with finicky ferns or rigorously demanding annuals and perennials, there are no better plants.

¶Gardeners living in colder climates should not be disheartened: there are hardy versions of cacti and succulents that survive even snowy conditions. In the Upper Peninsula of Michigan, Opuntia fragilis grow along the rocks of a south-facing mountain, surviving the subzero temperatures of winter because the snow is dry, and the snow melt and rains of spring because the quick-draining rocky soil never lets their roots become soggy. More tender varieties adapt well to outdoor life in containers, which allows you to move them to a protected place for the winter.

¶Many a person has bought just one cactus or succulent as a kind of joke, then later found the joke played out in windowsills, patios, and gardens filled with different types of these appealing plants. So be forewarned: Although you think just one plant couldn't hurt, you may be surprised at the number of cactus and succulents you suddenly own. You can really get stuck on these plants.

CHARACTERISTICS OF CACTI AND SUCCULENTS

Lumping cacti and succulents together as a group of plants may at first seem peculiar, for most cacti bristle with spiny armature while most succulents present a benign smooth look that is quite the opposite. They are linked together botanically because cacti and succulents share a mechanism for storing water in their cells, allowing them to endure an infrequent or minimal water supply. Unique cells in the stems, leaves, or roots collect and hold water, releasing it to the plant when needed.

¶There are about thirty thousand plants that can be called succulents. Of the many families of succulents, one, the Cactaceae, comprises cacti, in an astounding range of over two thousand species. The members of the Cactaceae family are stem succulents. Cells in the stems store water and enable photosynthesis to take place, as a leaf normally does. The other species of succulents are leaf succulents, whose swollen, fleshy leaves hold water for use when water is not available through the roots.

¶When you consider that deserts, arid mountains, and dry plateaus cover thirty-five percent of the earth's surface—some areas receiving as little as 2 inches of rainfall a year—it makes sense that a multitude of plant families would evolve similar strategies to survive with little water. Most succulents, except the cacti in the genus *Pereskia*, had little use for expansive leaves. Their surfaces lose, especially in hot climates, large amounts of water through an evaporative process called transpiration, when water from the soil is drawn up through the roots and out the pores in the leaves. Therefore, the solid shapes of cacti and their lack of leaves minimize water loss. The thick, fleshy leaves and stems of succulents also evolved to lower the loss of water through transpiration. All generalizations have exceptions, so don't be surprised if you see leaves on certain cacti. Many last only a short time, equivalent to a spring bloom, and then fall off.

¶Plants in low-rainfall areas also need to increase their ability to absorb water. Some plants have juicy, bulbous roots that swell to hold water during a brief season of rain. Others spread around them a wide circular mat of fine roots that absorb rain or dew. Still other plants have long tap roots, the larger ones reaching as deep as 30 feet for water. Knowing the root structure of the plant you own dictates the kind of container or planting space necessary to provide adequate room for healthy growth.

¶The limited or slow growth of cacti and succulents is timed to occur during the period of rainfall that provides water and nutrients. Most of these water-thrifty plants use the spring rains to put on growth and to flower, then they stop growing when rainfall ceases. Desert cacti need water through the springtime, then limited water in summer, and almost no water from late fall until spring, even though the plants may look shriveled. Once water is available, the plants burst into bloom. Without this withdrawal time, the plants suffer. Watering cacti and succulents in containers can be controlled, but caring for plants in perennial beds may be tricky, for you must select plants with similar watering requirements. Drought-tolerant plants and many native plants from dry summer areas make good neighbors.

WINTER HARDINESS

Don't think because snow covers your garden, you cannot grow cacti and succulents. The amount of water held in the leaves or stems makes most cacti and succulents susceptible to frosts, for the swelling of the freezing water molecules erupts and tears apart the cellular structure of the plants. Yet, many cacti and succulents survive in cold-winter areas with temperatures dropping below 0°F. Some varieties of cactus live in the snowy plains of Texas, others in the high desert areas of Peru, and many more on mountain slopes in the northern United States. Succulents come from all over the world, and many live in freezing climates.

BLOOM

From the blooming clusters of *Kalanchoe* to the graceful arching stalks of *Echeveria*, cacti and succulent flowers come in a variety of fascinating shapes. Colors range from pristine white to neon pinks, greens, and oranges. An entire year of color is possible if plants are chosen carefully; choose from Christmas cacti and *Lithops* in the winter, *Mammillaria* in the spring, *Echeveria* in the summer, and *Sedum* into the fall. When making selections, be aware that some larger cacti don't bloom in pots until they reach mature size, often taking fifty years or more, while others put on a display two or three times a year. On the other hand, some succulent flowers will stay in bloom for months.

¶Cacti and succulent flowers bloom both day and night and are pollinated by birds, bats, bees, moths and other insects. Some blooms disappear after a brief, one-day or one-night bloom while others are longer-lasting. If you desire plants with a long flowering period, make sure to inquire about this when buying plants.

SPINES

A number of succulents have spines, an adaptive feature to protect the juicy plants from hungry and thirsty animals, so just because a plant comes with thorns or spines, you can't assume it is a cactus. Yet, trying to identify an aloe from a cactus is simple because in the Cactaceae family, the spines grow in clusters from the center of areoles, small cushiony structures on the stems. *Euphorbia,* a genus of succulents that appear similar to cactus but are not genetically linked, have spines in patterns like cactus, but looking closely, you can see there are no areoles. Cactus spines can be thick, thin, almost microscopic, long, short, or fish hooked. The flowers also originate from the areoles. The spines keep away animals, and on plants with a thick pelt of fine spines, they also deflect the sun's rays. The number of spines and their configuration make up the fingerprint of each cactus variety. To identify a cactus, look closely at its spine structure.

SUCCULENTS

Succulents, the plants reflecting the meaning of their name, have juicy, water-filled stems, leaves, and roots, for like the camels of the desert, they must fill up with water when it is available. Distributed throughout the world, they have adapted to their environment with a stunning array of shapes, sizes, and colors, all finely tuned to survive periods of drought punctuated with bursts of rain. Because they come from such a broad range of habitats, there are succulents to suit the environment of your house and garden. Some dwell happily in the shade, some like full sun, and others want filtered sunlight. To cultivate succulents successfully, you need only match the cultural needs of the plant with your space and climate.

¶The stunning array of colors, forms, and textures of the petals of succulents wins them over to those gardeners with a sculptor's sensibility. Succulents formed with petals curled in rosettes, with very little or even no stem, include *Sempervivum, Crassula,* and *Echeveria,* among others. Some grow upright or lie prostrate on stems, such as *Haworthia, Kalanchoe, Sedum,* and *Ceropegia.* There are, however, some crossovers. Some *Crassula* are stemmed, and some *Aloes* can be rosettes, so you cannot categorize too generally. Lastly, there is a large group of succulents that send up stems resembling rocks, aptly called living stones.

¶Depending upon the variety, some succulents produce flamboyant, almost neon-bright flowers that blanket the garden in sizzling colors. The variety of blossom shapes, from bell-like, to daisy, to cluster heads, provides texture and color to the garden bed. The *Echeveria* have stems with bell-flowers in pink or orange and yellow. *Sedum spectabile* grows handsome heads of rusty red blooms. *Aloe saponaria* produces tall stems with 2-inch long bell-shaped flowers in clusters. Perhaps less showy than the splashy cactus blooms, still, succulent flowers provide long-lived garden pleasure, as the blooms may last for weeks and months instead of the ephemeral days of cactus blooms.

¶Those with less significant flowers dazzle with their leaf colors. For some reason, most books neglect to mention varieties with year-round ruby red leaves or another variety with celadon blue-green leaves with edges scalloped in pink. Green lobes have bright red borders. Shell pink types have contrasting burgundy tips. The magnificent leaf colors paint a bed with splashes of year-round color so you don't have to wait for the plant's yearly bloom.

¶The amount of sun a succulent receives affects its leaf color, whether the plant is grown inside or out. The more sun it gets, the more intense the color of its leaves. Grown indoors, plants fade if they are not placed in bright sunlight. Succulents that are normally highly colored become pale imitations of their sunnier selves if grown outdoors in filtered light.

CACTI

The ancient Greeks first used the word *kaktos,* meaning "spiny plant." Actually, what they were naming was not a cactus, but cardoon, a relative of the artichoke and a member of the sunflower family. Some two thousand years later, Linnaeus, who devised the botanical classification system we use today, applied the same word to describe the Cactaceae family.

¶Although you may think of this family as represented only by the desert varieties, cacti in their native habitats grow from Canada to South America. Although the majority grow under dry conditions, some types live in moist tropical forests, at sea level, and on top of mountains. Don't assume, therefore, that all cacti prefer blistering heat and only a smidgen of water.

¶It may be easiest to understand the needs of cacti by categorizing them as desert cacti or forest cacti. The desert types live in areas with low humidity and quick-draining, often sandy soil. The forest types, which include the epiphytic cacti that climb trees, live in humid areas with soil rich from rotted leaf matter. Once you know where your plant came from, you can fulfill its cultivation needs in your home or garden.

¶Also characteristic of cacti are the woolly, hairlike strands of fiber that grow out of the aureoles. Luxuriant or thin, the strands protect the plant from the searing, drying rays of the sun, almost a kind of protective clothing. Dew or other moisture that falls on the hair collects to drip down to the roots, adding another clever tool for gathering moisture.

¶Cacti occur in a number of shapes, and understanding these shapes helps identify the plants. *Opuntia*, the prickly pear and cholla cacti, have flat pads and spine cushions. Another group of cactus, recalling those in Western movies, has one or more upright or branched stems. These include the great *Carnegiea gigantea*, or saguaro. Barrel cacti grow as round balls, although some, when older, become more cylindrical. Forest cacti have long pendulous limbs with thin or thick succulent stems that look like leaves and are sometimes flat, sometimes angled. The limbs may be a long single stem or segmented like a crab's legs.

¶Cactus flowers are often exquisite, putting on a display that in size and color competes with the showiest orchids or spring-blooming bulbs. Some species bloom in the day, some at night, depending upon their pollinator. Over 450 cacti are night blooming, attracting bats and moths. Daytime flowers are pollinated by insects or birds. Many species are delicately fragrant.

¶Powerfully sun-sensitive, cactus flowers may not open at all or until later in the afternoon on gloomy days. Don't pluck off a flower when it closes, for it may be reacting to the setting sun and in the morning will unfold again. Although many blooms last only a day or a night, some reopen over a period of days.

¶If you want a cactus that flowers, you must choose carefully. Many cacti offered for sale are immature plants that eventually grow 20 feet or more and produce blossoms only when mature. Make a list of the appropriate species before you buy, find plants in bloom in the spring and summer, or check with the staff of a specialty plant store, nursery, or mail-order source.

Buying Plants

When you buy plants, be sure you know the scientific, or Latin, name of the plant. Common names are not consistent or accurate, and you may come home with a different plant from the one you intended. As an example, two succulents, an *Echeveria* and a *Sempervivum*, share the common name hens-and-chicks, so you'll find the right plant only if you have the Latin name of the one you want. The first part is the genus name; the second is the species. Cultivated varieties are indicated by a final element enclosed in single quote marks, as in *Sedum spurium* 'Tricolor,' a succulent. Hybrids of dissimilar genera or species are indicated by an "x" between the elements of the scientific name, such as x *Pachgerocereus orcuttii.*

¶Cacti and succulents are objects of such affection and scrutiny that breeders have been improving and multiplying the types commercially available. Thousands are found in nurseries, catalogues, and specialty garden stores. Local plant specialists offer types not available in another part of the country. Therefore, the plant recommendations given in this book are a guide and should be considered as a starting place. You will want to experiment and discover the plants best suited to your climate and soil.

¶Keep a record of when and where you bought your plants and how successfully they grow in your house or garden. A diary is one of the best tools to guarantee success in gardening.

ABOUT GROWING CACTI AND SUCCULENTS

Everyone can grow cacti and succulents, whether they have a sunny morning room, an outdoor patio, a sunny fire escape, or a garden. Grown in containers, indoors or out, or in the ground, these hardy plants reward the gardener with flowers, fruit, and an endlessly pleasing array of forms and textures. ¶Experienced growers fix you in the eye and let you know that doting gardeners kill their cacti and succulents by overwatering. The most important clue to successful growing of these plants is to be wary of your watering habits. Your watering schedule must depend upon whether the plant is a desert cactus or a forest cactus, the season—whether hot, dry summer or cold, damp winter—and the needs of the specific plant.

WATER

Understanding how a plant absorbs water helps the gardener deliver the water when the plant needs it, an essential aspect of caring for plants that can die from overwatering. In most plants, water carries nutrients from the soil or potting mix up through the roots and stem to the leaves. As it evaporates through pores in the leaves in a process called transpiration, the roots draw up more water, like straws sucking up liquid. Because cacti and succulents have roots, stems, and thick, fleshy leaves that minimize water loss from transpiration and also store water in the cells, they need less water than most other plants. The amount of water needed depends on the type and size of plant, the amount of direct sun it receives, the season and temperature, and whether the plant is in the ground or in a container.

¶A container-grown plant needs more frequent watering than one living in the ground, for the limited root space in the container restricts the amount of water available to the plant to collect and store. In determining a watering schedule, you must consider the size of the container and its material, whether plastic, terra-cotta, or glazed terra-cotta. A general rule is the smaller the container, the more frequent the watering. For a terra-cotta container, double the frequency. Terra-cotta containers are porous, so water evaporates through the sides of the container, while plastic pots help the potting mix retain moisture. Cold and rainy weather reduces transpiration, and as a result, plants need less water. Warm and windy days accelerate water use, and consequently, you must water plants more frequently.

¶In a container planted with a desert cactus or succulent, the potting mix should dry out before the plant is watered. Forest cacti should never dry out between waterings. Before you water, check the moisture content of the potting mix by probing the bottom of the container with your finger or a stick. If the soil mix sticks to your finger or the stick, it has not yet dried out completely and the plant doesn't need watering. Small, liftable containers can be checked using the "lightness" test. Practice hefting the container before and after watering so you can feel the difference. At first, you may not notice much of a change, but with time, you can tell from the relative lightness of the container whether you need to water immediately or to hold off for several days.

¶Always water thoroughly and well. When size allows, submerge the pot in a water-filled bucket or sink that is deep enough to allow the water to flow over the rim of the pot. Remove the pot when air bubbles no longer rise to the surface. This method permits the root ball to soak up sufficient water so that water doesn't simply stream down the sides of the dry root ball and exit the bottom hole. For containers too large or heavy for this maneuver, fill them with water, let drain, and repeat several times.

¶Many cacti and succulents benefit from being watered overhead, which washes and refreshes the plant. However, cactus topped with a mass of fibers called a cephalium and cacti and succulents with a delicate protective dusting of bloom lose their appearance with overhead watering. Make sure to water these types only at the base.

¶If a container sits in a saucer, empty it after watering. Standing water keeps the potting mix soggy, with the result that the roots rot and the plant dies. Place gravel in the saucer of a large pot that is too heavy to lift. This raises the bottom of the container above any standing water.

¶In contrast to plants in containers, plants in the ground have more room for the roots to spread and therefore a larger area from which to draw moisture from the soil. Consequently, these plants do not need to be watered as frequently as those in containers. Check the water content of the soil by digging down at least 2 to 3 inches. If the soil is dry, drench the plants thoroughly. Always water early in the day so plants are not wet overnight. Without a chance to dry out in the sun, water lodged in the crowns and leaves of the plants can encourage fungal disease.

¶For most cacti and succulents, watering should follow the natural growth cycle of the plants. This means that you can't expect to water automatically every two weeks throughout the year. Instead, along with starting to fertilize, watering should be increased in spring and summer, when the plant is growing, and should be decreased from fall through the winter, during the dormant period following the growth cycle of the plant.

¶During hot or windy weather, when plants use more water, small pots in direct sun may need watering every couple of days. Plants on slopes or in raised beds dry out faster than those on flat ground. Most cacti and succulents, particularly those in cold climates, need to dry out before the coldest weather in order to be protected from freezing temperatures. There are a number of plants that are exceptions to these guidelines, so make sure you learn their individual requirements.

¶The type of water you use impacts these plants. Well water with a high concentration of minerals or city water with chlorine or fluoride may leave spots of chemicals on the surface of plants. If your plants appear affected, you may want to set up a system for collecting rainwater or set out your tap water in the sunlight to dissipate some of the chemical content. As a cautionary measure, always water plants at their base and avoid splashing the stems and leaves.

LIGHT

Most cacti and succulents in pots are sun lovers that benefit from direct sunlight outside or three to four hours of sun inside. Not all of these plants, however, prefer full sunlight. Some varieties in their native habitat live in part shade, growing in the shadow of a larger plant for protection from the sun, and therefore may not perform well in a sunny windowsill. For indoor plants needing direct light, a south-facing window is ideal. A western or eastern exposure works as well in the winter. Watch the western exposure during the summer months, for the strong light may burn the foliage. The light in Tucson, Arizona, in the winter is quite different from the light in St. Paul, Minnesota, so be sure to compensate for your global location. Watch the reaction of your plants to the available light and move them in or out of it as seems appropriate for their growth. Remember to rotate containers periodically to keep the plants growing evenly.

¶Cacti and succulents newly arrived from a greenhouse or just sprouting tender new shoots need to acclimate for several days in bright light, not direct sunlight. Gradually move them into the direct sun, whether outside or in. Light green spots on foliage facing the sun indicate sunburn, actually the scorched epidermis of the plant, which, if extensive, can prove fatal.

¶Outdoors, most cacti and succulents grow better with full sun or at least four to five hours of bright sunlight. Again, check the requirements of your particular plants, for some, especially the forest cacti, prefer light shade. Some light exposures—a west-facing wall, for example—may be too hot for plants in containers. The potting mix can heat up to foundry levels, cooking out any moisture and baking the roots.

¶Cacti and succulents, as well as most other house plants, prosper with a short time outside in the summer. If you are summering your cacti outdoors, make sure to move them gradually into the light, and because they are inside most of the year, do not expose them to the full glare of harsh afternoon sun. They need filtered light, such as inside a lathhouse or underneath a tree.

TEMPERATURE AND FROST PROTECTION

As cacti and succulents grow all around the world, they naturally require different temperatures throughout the year. Adjusting your environment to their growth habit is crucial. For indoor plants from habitats with cool winters, low temperatures trigger dormancy, a stage essential to their life cycle, when they require little water and no fertilizer. Temperatures for winter-dormant plants should be on the cool side, from 50°F to 55°F. Whether your plants are normally kept indoors or moved inside to over-winter, keep them in this temperature range until the weather warms up in the spring, when growth begins or buds form. Then gradually move the plants to a warmer spot, whether indoors or out, and begin your fertilizing and watering regime.

¶Some cacti and succulents come from climates with warm winter days. Plants like forest cacti prefer a warm winter environment, around 60°F all year long. Keeping them indoors and continuing regular watering suit them perfectly.

¶Except for some species of *Opuntia* or *Sempervivum*, most cacti and succulents, because of the high water content in their leaves and stems, are frost tender and must be protected. Potted plants in an outdoor location are particularly quick to die from frostbite, so in cold winter climates they must be sheltered in sunny, protected locations where the temperature doesn't drop below the hardiness level, the lowest temperature that plants can tolerate. In general, keeping plants where the temperature is between 50°F and 60°F protects them and gives them a winter rest. Watering should be kept to a minimum. With some species, withholding water altogether is best for their health. The leaves may shrivel, but when you start watering again in the spring, they return to normal. Even though some cacti and succulents can survive colder temperatures, they show unsightly scars that may never heal.

Soils and Potting Mixes

Soil is a mixture of three particles—sand, silt, and clay—plus any organic matter. The silt, clay, and organic matter interact with water and provide nutrients to the plant roots. Sand, though chemically inert, also plays an important role in plant health. The largest in size of the particles, sand creates correspondingly large spaces between the soil particles, which contributes to fast drainage, high oxygen concentrations, and good vertical water movement. For cacti and succulents, this porosity of the soil is critical to keep roots from rotting and to allow plants to dry out between waterings. Some succulents can tolerate slightly wetter soil, but most desert cacti need soil that drains swiftly.

¶Forest cacti are the exception. Accustomed to life under trees, they require a potting mix rich in organic material such as peat moss or organic compost. Their roots need year-round moisture—they should not be soggy, but should never totally dry out. A well-formulated potting mix assists in retaining moisture. In the mildest of climates, where winter temperatures never drop below 42°F, forest cacti can be planted in the ground and trained to grow up trees.

¶For container plantings, use a good-quality potting mix made for cacti and succulents, which will ensure proper drainage. Commercial potting mixes have been sterilized to make them cleaner than decomposing organic materials for plants grown indoors. Top dressings such as pebbles, gravel, or even just plain sand covering the potting mix give a finished look to potted plants. Experiment with different top dressings to achieve the look you like. Top dressings don't need to be more than a half inch deep.

¶In regions with mild winter climates, where temperatures rarely drop below 32°F, cacti and succulents can successfully be grown outside, as long as you prepare the garden bed to provide excellent drainage.

¶Slow-draining soil or soil with a heavy clay base can cause roots to rot. A good garden soil crumbles easily in your hand. Before you plant, dig a test hole, fill it with water, and watch how the water drains out. For cacti and succulents, the water in the planting hole should drain out slowly but steadily. Excessively slow-draining soil must be improved with soil amendments to speed drainage. Try working in builder's sand and compost to improve the porosity of the soil. Also effective are mounded beds with soil raised 6 inches above the surrounding area to improve and assure quick-draining soil.

¶Prepare the garden soil two to three weeks before transplants are ready to set out. If the soil is so wet that it falls off the shovel in clumps, you need to wait to get started until the soil dries some or risk compacting the ground, making it rock hard. Compacted soil has less oxygen, so the roots suffer from oxygen deprivation and the plants will not grow successfully.

¶First remove existing plant material such as weeds or plants that you no longer want to grow there. Add 4 inches of organic compost and, if necessary, 2 inches of builder's sand. Using a shovel, a spade, or a machine such as a Rototiller, turn over the soil to a depth of 12 to 18 inches. Water the turned soil and allow any undesirable seeds in the ground to sprout. When the ground is damp but not soggy, remove the weeds once again. Break up any clods with a hoe or shovel and rake the surface smooth for planting.

FERTILIZERS

The major nutrients needed for plant growth are nitrogen, phosphorus, and potassium (N, P, and K respectively). A plant removes these nutrients from the soil and uses them to grow. Adding fertilizer to the soil replaces the missing or depleted nutrients and allows the plant to continue its growth. Because nutrient requirements are greatest during periods of growth, fertilize garden beds when you are preparing them for planting. That way, new plants will have fertilizer available to them.

¶The percentages of each nutrient, in the order nitrogen-phosphorus-potassium, are listed on commercial fertilizers. An NPK formula of 10-10-10, for example, has equal amounts of nitrogen, phosphorus, and potassium. Most experts recommend a low-nitrogen formula, such as 5-10-10, for growing cacti and succulents in the ground. A pelleted, slow-release, low-nitrogen formula can be applied to the soil before planting according to the directions on the container. Established plants benefit from a yearly addition of low-nitrogen fertilizer worked into the soil around their roots.

¶Potting mix is a sterile medium, so container plants need a different fertilizing procedure from plants in garden beds. Discussing the best method to fertilize potted plants brings out all the experts, each with a different opinion. However, a professional grower suggests using an all-purpose liquid formula diluted one half strength. Find a fertilizer with a formula of 10-10-10. A 20-20-20 can be used as well. Unless the needs of a specific plant dictate otherwise, begin fertilizing containers every two weeks in the spring when the weather warms up and the plants show growth. As summer draws to a close, growth slows, and the plant no longer needs the extra boost of fertilizer, so plan to

stop fertilizing at summer's end. If plants begin to show excessive growth under this regime, then cut the formula in half again.

¶Because cacti and succulents naturally grow slowly, too much fertilizer causes gangly growth that may weaken the plant, leaving it susceptible to disease. Many nurseries sell plants with a slow-release fertilizer already applied to the planting mix, advising the new owner not to fertilize monthly.

Repotting

Although succulents are a breeze to repot, both the novice and the expert approach handling cacti with some trepidation, and even the most experienced expect to be pricked. Certain tips can help protect the wary gardener from too much discomfort. Long-nosed pliers or tongs allow a small container to be plucked from a group of containers, confounding the reach of neighboring cacti. Heavy leather gloves, in particular, goatskin gloves impervious to thorns, help thwart the penetration of spines. When handling most species of *Opuntia*, fine barbed filaments of the glochids stick in gloves and are almost impossible to remove. Try using disposable rubber gloves instead.

¶The time to repot is when the plant overflows its container or when there are so many offshoots that the plant has lost its shape. For best results, repot after the blossoming finishes. You never want to move a plant from a small container into a much larger container, but to increase the size gradually, about 2 inches larger in circumference.

¶When repotting, have handy a new container, fertilizer, and fresh potting mix. Water the plant the day before. For a small plant, fold over the top of a paper bag so it is double strength or nest two equal-sized bags, and slip over the top of the cactus. With larger plants, fold several sheets of newspaper to make a strip about 6 inches wide that you can wrap around the plant. Wearing gloves, place the covered or wrapped plant on its side, and tap the container on the bottom and sides, rotating it to loosen the root ball. Slide out the root ball, using the paper bag or newspaper for protection until you can grasp the root ball. Examine the roots and trim off any brown and desiccated dead roots.

¶Add enough new potting mix to the new container so the top of the root ball comes 2 inches from the rim of the container. With the plant centered in the middle of its new container, fill in around the sides with fresh potting mix. Tamp the mix firmly around the root ball, making sure the plant is set evenly in the container and the top of the root ball remains 2 inches below the rim. Top-dress, if you wish, with stones, shells, gravel, or sand. Water well.

¶Let the plant rest out of direct light without watering for one week for a small container, or up to two weeks for a larger one. Gradually return the container to its original location. Don't fertilize until next spring. If any roots have been damaged in the repotting, the fertilizer can kill them, which will affect the overall health of the plant.

PROPAGATION

On the whole, cacti and succulents propagate easily, and half the fun of growing them is creating many new plants for your own use or as gifts. You will have the greatest success during the spring growing season. Offsets, known in the trade as "pups," that grow as clusters off the mother plant can easily be separated and rooted. For cacti, protect your hands and remove the offset from the main plant by twisting it gently. If

it doesn't twist off, use a sharp knife to cut it away. Succulents can be cut or twisted off the main stem. Don't use clippers, for they crush and bruise the plant flesh instead of slicing it cleanly.

¶Let the cactus or succulent cutting dry out and form a skin, or callus, by leaving it in the open air, but not in direct sunlight. After several days, depending upon the size of the offshoot, a dry, brown skin forms over the area separated from the main plant. After the callus forms, set the offshoot into a small pot filled with a cactus potting mix that has been thoroughly moistened. Let the container sit out of direct light for two to three weeks. Check to see if the roots have formed by pulling up very gently on the new plant. Resistance means the plant has made roots. If the plant has rooted, begin weekly watering, gradually moving the plant to brighter light. If roots have not yet formed, continue to check it weekly until it roots.

¶Succulents and forest cacti root easily from stem cuttings. Find a narrow stem of younger shoots—the older woody shoots are less successful—and remove it with a sharp blade so you have a clean cut. Dust the end with rooting hormone and let the cutting sit until a callus forms. Then, root the cutting in a small pot filled with cactus potting mix, and proceed as with offshoots.

¶Leaves of succulents can be rooted to form new plants. Twist or cut off the largest leaf and dust it with rooting hormone. Let it dry for several days and then place the lower third of the leaf into a small pot of cactus potting mix and proceed as for cactus offshoots.

Pests and Diseases

Cacti and succulents, although not impervious to disease and pests, certainly are less susceptible than many plants. Careful weekly inspection helps to halt an insect invasion before it becomes critical. Watch in particular for scale, which looks like a brown wart on the surface of the plant and may come in clumps of several at a time. Mealy bugs and woolly aphids both look like bits of white fluff, but don't confuse them with perlite, the mineral granules in potting soil, which can get stuck on cactus spines. The best treatment for a small plant is to spray it vigorously with water in the morning to wash away the pests.

¶Slugs and snails seem to realize the full meaning of the word *succulent*, devouring the juicy, tender flesh, eating around spines as necessary. Plants in containers can be protected by a strip of copper wrapped around the base of the container. The copper gives a slight shock to slugs and snails when they try to cross it. Check garden plants early in the spring when slugs and snails are the most ravenous. Perusing the garden bed in the dark of night with a flashlight can yield a bountiful harvest of slugs and snails. Place the varmints in a plastic bag, close tightly, and discard.

¶Cacti and succulents are vulnerable to fungal diseases and rot. An affected plant generally turns brown at the base. The disease gradually works its way up the plant. The only cure is to cut off the plant above the diseased area, allow a callus to form on the healthy cutting, and then repot it. Make sure to discard the diseased plant and potting mix. If a plant in the ground rots, check whether the soil is draining fast enough. Dig out the affected plant. Remove all the soil in a circle around its roots and discard. Add new soil, along with amendments such as builder's sand and well-rotted compost, to improve the drainage, and replant.

SPINES

Although some succulents have spiky protrusions, cacti have spines that are needle sharp and so numerous they cover most of the surface of the plant. Just a gentle nudge of a spine can give you a painful poke. Wily, hooked spines can quickly take a hold and are difficult to disengage without hurting yourself or the plant. The small spines in tufts of certain *Opuntia* can be dislodged from the plant by the slightest draft. When handling cactus, remember to use thick thorn-proof gloves. If a hooked spine impales you, use a stick or a pencil to pull the hook out in the direction in which it lodged. For finer spines, try pulling them out with cellophane tape. Small children can easily tumble into plants, so consider this potential hazard when planting cactus and succulents in the ground or arranging containers.

A WINDOWSILL

GARDEN

For those gardeners who have yet to successfully grow an indoor house plant, cacti and succulents may be the answer. It is often the case where house plants shrivel and die, cacti

and succulents will thrive. Unlike house plants, which often come from the lush and low light of the jungle, cacti and succulents are adjusted to periods of low water and exposure to sun and enjoy basking in the dry environment of heated rooms. They prefer less, rather than more, water. They are so slow growing that they won't outgrow their spaces, so you can plan to keep the plants in your chosen location for a long time. ❧ Many large nurseries, outlets, and catalogues offer plants in 2- to 4-inch pots at prices so reasonable that you can fill several windows without needing a large budget. If possible, purchase cacti and succulents in spring and summer, when the plants are in bloom, so you can enjoy the lavish and spectacular rewards of the plants' growth over the previous year. Your new residents need time to adjust to their surroundings. Do not place them immediately in a sunny windowsill. Instead, situate plants away from direct light and gradually move them closer to the window. The plants may have been raised in a greenhouse without direct sunlight, and like winter-tender skin, they need to be exposed slowly to the sun to avoid sunburn. ❧ Remember that the level and intensity of the sun's rays change from season to season. A west-facing window may provide the perfect light for your plants in December but may be too hot in August. Observe how your plants perform, and be prepared to change their location if the climate becomes inhospitable.

A CHILD'S GARDEN

Children find small cacti and succulents as beguiling as little action figures. They appear friendly and charming, and their almost indestructible nature makes them good training for future gardeners, although a warning about avoiding the spines is necessary. ¶ Visit nurseries several times during spring and summer to buy a mix of cacti and succulents in continuous bloom if possible. Plants available in the suggested varieties come with blooms in a rainbow of colors, from snow white to fire-engine red, and in sizes from ¼-inch to 3-inches tall. Prune back the succulents to keep them suitably sized to the window-ledge space. Children can pot up the cuttings to give to their friends (see propagation, pages 38–39). ¶ Because the containers are small, the plants need to be watered more often than plants in larger containers. Grouping them in a box keeps the soil temperature low and helps preserve moisture. Consider placing the containers in a large, glazed saucer filled with sand to make watering easy and avoid spills. Marking the calendar with watering and fertilizing dates is not only handy but fun for children. ¶ **HOW TO DO IT** ¶ Gradually introduce the plants to a windowsill with at least three hours of direct sun. In the growing season, from March through September, water every one to two weeks. In fall and winter, from October through February, water every two to three weeks. In hot weather, you may need to increase watering. Fertilize, after you water, once a month from March through August with an all-purpose liquid fertilizer diluted half strength and applied according to the directions on the container.

Assorted cacti and succulents
especially Mammillaria, Echinocereus, Sempervivum, Rebutia, Notocactus, and Echeveria, in 2 to 4-inch pots

❧

What You Need
All-purpose liquid fertilizer
diluted half strength

❧

Light
3 hours direct morning or afternoon sun

❧

Watering Schedule
Every 1 to 2 weeks from March through September, every 2 to 3 weeks from October through February, more often in hot weather

❧

Fertilizing Schedule
Once a month from March through August

❧

Hardiness
To 50°F

❧

When Blooms Appear
Spring or summer depending upon variety

❧

Haworthia fasciata, Fairy Washboard

The green-and-white zebra-striped leaves of this small succulent make the plant a lively addition to any north-facing windowsill—perfect for jazzing up a space without direct sunlight. The tapered, pointed leaves, growing in rosettes, look like the wavy arms of an underwater sea creature. With a stretch of your imagination, the green-and-white stripes are reminiscent of the surface of an old-time washboard. ¶ Haworthia, from South Africa, is a member of the lily family. This species rarely grows taller than 7 or 8 inches. Enjoy the patterned leaves, but don't hold great expectations for the bloom. The flowers are gray-white, small, and bell shaped, rising above the plant on a thin stem. Some growers prefer to pinch off the bloom stalks as they emerge, letting the plant use its energy for leaf growth. Try lining up several of these plants along a north-facing windowsill for a handsome arrangement. ¶ **HOW TO DO IT** ¶ Place the plants on a windowsill with bright light but no direct sunlight. In the growing season, from March through September, water every one to two weeks. In late fall and winter, from October through February, water every two to three weeks. In hot weather, you may need to increase watering. Fertilize, after you water, once a month from March through August with an all-purpose liquid fertilizer diluted half strength and applied according to the directions on the container.

Fairy Washboard
Haworthia fasciata

What You Need
*All-purpose liquid fertilizer
diluted half strength*

Light
Bright light without direct sun

Watering Schedule
*Every 1 to 2 weeks from March
through September, every 2 to 3 weeks
from October through February,
more often in hot weather*

Fertilizing Schedule
Once a month from March through August

Hardiness
To 50°F

When Blooms Appear
Insignificant blooms in early summer

Lithops, living-stones

The succulent family is full of surprises, and one of its most astonishing members, the Mesembryanthemum family, has adapted a physiological structure and coloring to survive the extremely dry conditions of its South African home. Their two fleshy leaves—all that make up these miniature plants—grow only 1 to 2 inches in diameter and, at their tallest, are about 1 inch. This structure allows them to store a maximum of water with a minimum of loss. Lithops derives from the Greek and means "stones." The form and coloring of these plants cleverly mimic their native rocky surroundings, disguising and hiding them from thirsty and hungry creatures. ¶ During the growth period, the fissure between the two leaves opens to expose two tiny new leaves. The old leaves gradually die back and fade in color as their moisture is absorbed by the plant—water economy to be sure. The new leaves carry the true color of the stones. The flowers emerge from the center of the cleft, and look like a yellow or white dandelion flower set into rocks. ¶ Lithops send out a long, thin root and grow the most successfully in deep containers. Unlike many other succulents, Lithops grow in winter, so start watering with greater frequency, though still sparsely, in December. ¶ **HOW TO DO IT** ¶ Gradually introduce the plants to a windowsill with at least four hours of direct sun. In the growing season, from December through April, water sparingly every one to two weeks. From May through November, water every two to three weeks. In hot weather, you may need to increase watering. Fertilize, after you water, once a month from December through April with an all-purpose liquid fertilizer diluted half strength and applied according to the directions on the container.

Living-Stones
Lithops

What You Need
All-purpose liquid fertilizer diluted half strength

Light
4 hours direct morning or afternoon sun

Watering Schedule
Sparingly every 1 to 2 weeks from December through April, every 2 to 3 weeks May through November, more often in hot weather

Fertilizing Schedule
Once a month from December through April

Hardiness
To 45°F, keep temperatures above 55°F

When Blooms Appear
Any time of year depending upon variety

CEPHALOCEREUS SENILIS, MEXICAN OLD-MAN CACTUS

The fuzzy, bearded look of this cactus comes from the woolly covering that filters out harsh rays of the sun. The cephalium is the woolly mass that emerges from the top of the cactus, the growing part, and where, as a mature plant, the white blooms are formed. Fibers also emerge from the areoles along the sides of the plant. ¶ Full-grown specimens stretch up to 40 to 50 feet. At that height, they are estimated to be over two hundred years old. The growth is leisurely enough that you won't need to make a hole in your roof to keep your plant indoors. Unfortunately, only mature plants bloom, so don't expect flowers on your windowsill-sized cactus. ¶ In its native Mexico, old-man cactus grows in hot areas, where the nights are cool in winter. Keep it in a cool room during the winter and water sparingly during the summer. ¶ You may come across two similar cacti from South America, South American old-man-of-the-mountains, *Oreocereus celsianus,* and old-man-of-the-Andes, *O. trollii, also covered with dense fibers. These can be substituted for Mexican old-man cactus.* ¶ **HOW TO DO IT** ¶ Gradually introduce the plant to a windowsill with at least three hours of direct sun each day. In the growing season, from March through September, water about every one to two weeks. In fall and winter, from October through February, water every two to three weeks. Water carefully at the base of the plant so you don't displace any of the hair, which, once lost, does not regrow. In hot weather, you may need to increase watering. Fertilize, after you water, once a month from March through August with an all-purpose fertilizer diluted half strength and applied according to the directions on the container.

Old-Man Cactus
Cephalocereus senilis,
Oreocereus celsianus, O. trollii,

❧

What You Need
All-purpose liquid fertilizer
diluted half strength

❧

Light
3 hours direct morning or afternoon sun

❧

Watering Schedule
Every 1 to 2 weeks from March
through September, every 2 to 3 weeks
from October through February,
more often in hot weather

❧

Fertilizing Schedule
Once a month from March
through August

❧

Hardiness
To 55°F

❧

When Blooms Appear
None

❧

ECHINOCEREUS

The gorgeously blooming species in this genus go by a number of common names, some confusingly applied to several different cacti. Echinos, a Greek word, has been generally translated by cacti aficionados as "hedgehog," a name sometimes applied to the whole group or specifically to E. pentalophus or E. adustus. Sometimes, to add to the confusion, it is used to refer to Echinopsis, a separate genus. Until you see one of the blooms, it is hard to believe that such a round, prickly (hence the name hedgehog) plant can burst out with a blossom 3 inches across and 4 inches tall. ¶ Filled with these cacti, your windowsill in spring will have a fireworks of blossoms in white, red, pink, pink and white, yellow, or orange, depending upon the variety, which hover over the plant for several days. ¶ **HOW TO DO IT** ¶ Gradually introduce the plants to a windowsill with at least three hours of direct sun each day. In the growing season, from March through September, water every one to two weeks. In fall and winter, from October through February, water every two to three weeks. In hot weather, you may need to increase watering. Fertilize, after you water, once a month from March through August with an all-purpose liquid fertilizer diluted half strength and applied according to the directions on the container.

Assorted Echinocereus,
especially E. gentryi, E. rigidissimus, E. pentalophus, E. salm-dyckianus, *and* E. subdenudata, *in 2- to 4-inch pots*

❧

What You Need
All-purpose liquid fertilizer diluted half strength

❧

Light
3 hours direct morning or afternoon sun

❧

Watering Schedule
Every 1 to 2 weeks from March through September, every 2 to 3 weeks from October through February, more often in hot weather

❧

Fertilizing Schedule
Once a month from March through August

❧

Hardiness
To 50°F

❧

When Blooms Appear
Spring or summer depending upon variety

❧

MAMMILLARIA

Mammillaria, *wildly popular with beginners as well as sophisticated collectors, can be found in many nurseries and hardware stores. With over 350 species available, you have quite a selection in form and in bloom color, from cream to yellow to pink and red. There are those covered with white fibers, those with hooked spines, and those with such closely knit spines they are called huggables because they don't poke you.* ¶ *Part of the charm of these cacti lies in the profusion of blooms crowded around the crown of the* plant, which looks as if it were wearing a chic bonnet. Flowers begin to appear at the turn of the spring equinox and last about a week, so this is a good time to begin shopping for a plant. Check the nursery throughout the spring and summer for the availability of flowering plants to bring home in order to extend the bloom season of your windowsill garden. ¶ If a plant grows larger than you wish, cut off one or more of the offsets from the mother plant in the spring. Let it dry for several days, then set in moist cactus potting mix (see pages 38–39). Within several weeks, it will root. ¶ **HOW TO DO IT** ¶ Gradually introduce the plants to a windowsill with at least three hours of direct sun each day. In the growing season, from March through September, water every one to two weeks. In fall and winter, from October through February, water every two to three weeks. In hot weather, you may need to increase watering. Fertilize, after you water, once a month from March through August with an all-purpose fertilizer diluted half strength and applied according to the directions on the container.

Assorted Mammillaria
such as Mammilaria bocasana,
M. pringlei, M. prolifera,
M. spinosissima, *and*
M. zeilmanniana, *in 2-to 4-inch pots*

❦

What You Need
*All-purpose liquid fertilizer
diluted half strength*

❦

Light
3 hours direct morning or afternoon sun

❦

Watering Schedule
*Every 1 to 2 weeks from March
through September, every 2 to 3 weeks
from October through February,
more often in hot weather*

❦

Fertilizing Schedule
Once a month from March through August

❦

Hardiness
To 50°F

❦

When Blooms Appear
Spring or summer depending upon variety

❦

INDOOR

POTTED

GARDENS

W hat makes cacti and succulents particularly appealing as house plants is their structural elegance. Like pieces of sculpture to be admired in different

lights, these plants are as valued as any modern sculpture for their clean lines and restrained beauty. ❧ Group plants to underscore the similarity in their forms, tonalities, and blooms, or use them singly for dramatic effect. A focal point, such as the end of a hallway or staircase, is a good site for a cluster of tall cacti. Brightly lit corners make an effective location to display the strong shapes of large plants. Floodlights behind plants give them striking impact. ❧ Choose the location based not only on the cultural needs of the plants, but also on the relationship between their potential size and the space available. Some of the cascading cacti or succulents grow to sizable proportions and can handle a large space. A diminutive hearts a-tangle, with its delicately shaped leaves, can inhabit a more confined area. ❧ Hanging plants near windows, stairways, skylights, or doorways provides dramatic accents, but make sure they are out of the way of foot traffic. Bumping into a cactus can be surprising and painful and succulents and forest cacti can lose blooms or stems. ❧ For indoor plants, you need glazed dishes under the containers to catch draining water and prevent it from staining wood surfaces. Water judiciously and add pebbles to the dishes to lift containers above any standing water.

SCHLUMBERGERA BRIDGESII HYBRIDS, CHRISTMAS CACTUS

There is no more cheerful sight at the holiday season than the winter-blooming Christmas cactus, with its arching branches tipped with bright red or pink blossoms. Choose from hybrids with short 6-inch branches or standards 3 to 4 feet in diameter, both dripping with blooms. Although dozens of glorious hybrid varieties are featured in nurseries and catalogues, a great deal of mystery and myth surrounds the Christmas cactus, and many gardeners steer clear of it because the various instructions for making it bloom seem so contradictory. Some gardeners suggest putting the plant in a closet after it blooms. Others insist it should be placed in a dark corner from September to Thanksgiving and should not be watered. What's a poor gardener to do with all this advice? ¶ First of all, remember that this is one of the forest cacti. It needs a rich, porous potting mix with peat moss and sand, rather than regular cactus potting mix. Christmas cactus also requires regular watering and fertilizing, particularly when it starts to form buds. As for some types of orchids, the cool evening temperatures and short days of autumn trigger bloom formation. In the summer, you can leave the plant outside in filtered sunlight until frost threatens. Then move it to a cool area, at about 50°F, until buds begin to form. Introduce it gradually to warmer temperatures to avoid bud drop. If you keep it inside just before bud formation, place it in a room that is dark for twelve to fourteen hours. ¶ **HOW TO DO IT** ¶ Place the plant in an area with bright light but no direct sunlight. Water every one to two weeks year-round, making sure the potting mix never totally dries out. In hot weather, you may need to increase watering. Fertilize year-round every two weeks, after you water, with an all-purpose liquid fertilizer diluted half strength and applied according to the directions on the container. In fall, keep the plant in a location with cool (50°F) evening temperatures and twelve to fourteen hours of darkness a day until buds begin to form.

Christmas Cactus
Schlumbergera bridgesii *hybrids*

What You Need
*All-purpose liquid fertilizer
diluted half strength*

Light
*Bright light without direct sun indoors,
filtered sunlight outdoors*

Watering Schedule
*Every 1 to 2 weeks year-round,
more often in hot weather*

Fertilizing Schedule
Every 2 weeks year-round

Hardiness
To 45°F

When Blooms Appear
*From November through December
or later depending upon variety*

CEROPEGIA WOODII, HEARTS A-TANGLE

When you try to disentangle the long hanging stems of this succulent, you will appreciate the humor of one of its common names, for the heart-shaped leaves strung in pairs down the stem catch and tangle like star-crossed lovers. Otherwise well behaved, these plants rarely outgrow their containers—though the stems of older plants reach as long as 4 feet. The thick leaves and water-storing tubers enable this South African vine to thrive in its native habitat. ¶ Hearts a-tangle grow best in bright or filtered sunlight. As with many succulents, the amount of sun they receive affects the color of the leaves. Brighter light intensifies the colors; dimmer light pales them. Look for 1-inch-long, trumpet-shaped, pinkish purple blooms in spring or early summer. Tubers sometimes form along the strands. When snipped off, they root easily to make new plants. ¶ **HOW TO DO IT** ¶ Place the plant in an area with bright light but no direct sunlight. In the growing season, from March through September, water every one to two weeks. In fall and winter, from October through February, water every two to three weeks. In hot weather, you may need to increase watering. Fertilize, after you water, once a month from March through August with an all-purpose fertilizer diluted half strength and applied according to the directions on the container.

Hearts A-Tangle
Ceropegia woodii

What You Need
*All-purpose liquid fertilizer
diluted half strength*

Light
Bright light without direct sun

Watering Schedule
*Every 1 to 2 weeks from March
through September, every 2 to 3 weeks
from October through February,
more often in hot weather*

Fertilizing Schedule
*Once a month from March
through August*

Hardiness
To 50°F
When Blooms Appear
Spring to summer

Epiphyllum hybrids, Orchid Cactus

Once you have seen the silky petals and huge blossoms, it's no mystery why the plants in this genus are called orchid cacti. In their native culture of the tropical Americas, they grow as rampant vines, sometimes as long as 225 feet. Extensively hybridized since the nineteenth century, the plants can be maintained tamely in a hanging basket as they throw off great clumps of 4-inch-wide blooms in a glorious variety of reds, pinks, yellows, oranges, whites, and shades in between. ¶ In the summer, orchid cacti benefit from a stint outside in a lathhouse or under a tree with filtered sunlight, although this is not essential. The leaves begin to take on a reddish tinge when in the sun. Because these plants come from tropical jungles, they need to be protected from even a hint of frost. Watch out for slugs and snails, which find the succulent leaves of this plant particularly delicious. ¶ There is some confusion over the name, since Epiphyllum hybrids are made by crossing a number of varieties. You may find them listed under Phyllocactus. ¶ **HOW TO DO IT** ¶ Place the plant in an area with bright or filtered sunlight. In the growing season, from March through October, water about every five days. In late fall and winter, from November through February, water every seven to ten days. In hot weather, you may need to increase watering. Do not let the plant ever dry out completely. In the summer, move the plant outside to a lathhouse or another area where it receives filtered sunlight. Fertilize, after you water, every two weeks from March through September with an all-purpose liquid fertilizer diluted half strength and applied according to the directions on the container.

Orchid Cactus
Epiphyllum *hybrids, sometimes called* Phyllocactus

What You Need
All-purpose liquid fertilizer, diluted half strength

Light
Bright light or filtered sunlight indoors, filtered sunlight outdoors

Watering Schedule
Every 5 days from March through October, every 7 to 10 days from November through February, more often in hot weather

Fertilizing Schedule
Every 2 weeks from March through September

Hardiness
To 45°F

When Blooms Appear
Spring or early summer depending upon variety

KALANCHOE BLOSSFELDIANA

These cheerful succulents with glossy, dark green leaves edged in red can be seen displayed in many florist shops and nurseries. Although they are commonly available, their virtue lies in the long-lived, 2- to 4-inch-wide sprays of small, bell-shaped blossoms in splashes of red, salmon, pink, yellow, or white. This species has been hybridized so dozens of different plants are available, from stout dwarf types just 6 inches high to those 14 inches tall with a spread just as wide. This handsome plant tolerates different light levels, from direct sun to dim corners, so a north-facing window gives enough light to satisfy its needs. ¶ The plants often come in pots wrapped in foil. Some gardeners discard the foil and slip the plant into a cache pot, but others leave it on. If you do so, do not allow the excess water to sit in the bottom of the wrapping. If you summer your Kalanchoe outside, maintain a vigilant watch for slugs and snails, which adore the tender leaves. ¶ **HOW TO DO IT** ¶ Place the plant in an area with bright light but no direct sunlight. In the growing season, from March through September, water every one to two weeks. In late fall and winter, from October through February, water every two to three weeks. In hot weather, you may need to increase watering. Fertilize, after you water, once a month from March through August with an all-purpose fertilizer diluted half strength and applied according to the directions on the container.

Kalanchoe blossfeldiana

What You Need
*All-purpose liquid fertilizer
diluted half strength*

Light
Bright light without direct sun

Watering Schedule
*Every 1 to 2 weeks from March
through September, every 2 to 3 weeks
from October through February,
more often in hot weather*

Fertilizing Schedule
*Once a month from March
through August*

Hardiness
To 45°F

When Blooms Appear
*Winter to early spring depending
upon variety*

APOROCACTUS FLAGELLIFORMIS, RATTAIL CACTUS

For those of you shuddering at the thought of these toothy rodents, relax, for this friendly plant merely has hanging rat-tail-thick limbs. When the plant is young, bright pink-red blooms start to appear at the top. As the plant matures, the 2-inch-long blossoms cover each branch from top to bottom. The limbs of this plant, perfect for a hanging basket, can grow to 6 feet long. ¶ Like orchid cacti, rattail cacti need a rich potting mix and should never be allowed to dry out as much as desert cacti, though they should not be as wet as forest cacti. A regular spring fertilizing schedule ensures a generous bloom. Unlike some cacti, which prefer cramped quarters in pots, these cacti should be repotted every year. If a plant grows too long for its allotted space, you can simply trim the "tails," let them callus for two to three days, and then set them into potting mix to start new plants (see pages 38–39). ¶ **HOW TO DO IT** ¶ Place the plant in an area with four or more hours of direct sunlight each day. In the growing season, from March through September, water every five days. In fall and winter, from October through February, water every seven to ten days. In hot weather, you may need to increase watering. Do not ever let the plant dry out completely. In the summer, move the plant outside to a lathhouse or where it receives filtered sunlight. Fertilize, after you water, every two weeks from March through September with an all-purpose liquid fertilizer diluted half strength and applied according to the directions on the container.

Rattail Cactus
Aporocactus flagelliformis

What You Need
All-purpose liquid fertilizer, diluted half strength
❧
Light
4 or more hours direct morning or afternoon sun
❧
Watering Schedule
Every 7 to 10 days from October through February, every 5 days in warm weather, more often in hot weather
❧
Fertilizing Schedule
Every 2 weeks from March through September
❧
Hardiness
To 37°F
❧
When Blooms Appear
Spring and summer
❧

Senecio Rowleyanus, String-of-Beads

This succulent looks like its common name, with small green balls joined together by a thin filament of a stem. A mature plant reaches 2 to 3 feet long, making it a dramatic plant for a hanging container. The ¼-inch beads are actually the plant's leaves swollen with a supply of water. ¶ It's hard to imagine that this quirky plant, a member of the huge Compositae family, is kin to sunflowers and the perennial dusty miller. What gives away its family ties are the small, creamy yellow, daisylike flowers slightly perfumed like carnations and appearing in summer. As for most of the succulents, pinching a stem and rooting a bead results in a new plant. ¶ **HOW TO DO IT** ¶ Place the plant in an area with bright light but no direct sunlight. In the growing season, from March through September, water every one to two weeks. In fall and winter, from October through February, water every two to three weeks. In hot weather, you may need to increase watering. Fertilize, after you water, every one to two weeks from March through August with an all-purpose liquid fertilizer diluted half strength and applied according to the directions on the container.

String-of-Beads
Senecio rowleyanus

What You Need
*All-purpose liquid fertilizer
diluted half strength*

Light
Bright light without direct sun

Watering Schedule
*Every 1 to 2 weeks from March
through September, every 2 to 3 weeks
from October through February,
more often in hot weather*

Fertilizing Schedule
*Every 1 to 2 weeks from March
through August*

Hardiness
To 45°F

When Blooms Appear
Summer

OUTDOOR

POTTED

GARDENS

Cactus and succulents, grown in pots on terraces, decks, and verandas, benefit from fresh air and sunshine. They can also be relocated easily. Plants in pots can be protected from the cold by being moved to a sunny shelter in winter areas where temperatures fall below 50°F. During the warm weather, they can be arranged to benefit from the changing sun exposure or to highlight their bloom. Don't let your container gardens become boring. Shift plants around to try combinations of different textures, heights, and colors. Experiment with fun containers such as colorful olive oil cans or flea market finds. ❧ For gardeners in cold winter climates who would like to place plants in garden beds, pots make it possible to set out an assortment of plants. A covering of mulch conceals the edges of the dug-in pots. When chilly temperatures threaten, the pots can be lifted and taken to cover. For convenience, you can slip containers into slightly larger pots in the ground. When you remove the plants in the fall, leave the outer containers hidden under mulch to ride out the winter until you replace the plants in the spring. ❧ Plants in pots exposed to sun and wind dry out quicker than those sheltered indoors, so monitor their potting mix regularly. If the weather becomes blistering hot or tempestuously windy, the soil in the pots dries out fast, so adjust your watering schedule to the conditions. Check the mix before you water, remembering not to soak your cactus and succulents absentmindedly at the same time you are drenching your begonias.

ALOE VERA, MEDICINAL ALOE

This succulent has the reputation of being a veritable medicine chest. The plant is also described as a gift from Venus, the Roman goddess of beauty, for bringing luster to hair and smoothness to skin. Cleopatra's exquisite complexion is credited to Aloe vera. Folk remedies prescribe sipping an infusion of the leaves for improved digestion and rubbing the peeled leaf over burned skin to relieve and help heal the wound. ¶ Browsing a drugstore, you'll discover a surprising number of products that list aloe as an ingredient. The plant is used to produce antibiotics, astringents, a pain reliever, and even substances that speed healing. All you need to do is keep a potted plant near your kitchen door in case of accidental burns. Simply slice off a sliver of the plant and rub over the affected area. ¶ The plant has plenty of other merits. The stemless gray-green leaves grow to 2 feet long and point upward in a V-shape. Tall flower stalks carry bursts of bright yellow flowers. Although as drought resistant as most succulents, this plant stays particularly handsome when well watered throughout the year. Aloe vera is also found under the name A. barbadensis. ¶ **HOW TO DO IT** ¶ Place the plant outside in an area with direct sunlight for four to six hours or more each day. In the growing season, from March through September, water every one to two weeks. In fall and winter, from October through February, water every two to three weeks. Move the plant to a protected location when the temperature drops below 45°F. Fertilize, after you water, once a month from March through August with an all-purpose liquid fertilizer diluted half strength and applied according to the directions on the container.

Medicinal Aloe
Aloe vera, *sometimes labeled*
A. barbadensis

What You Need
*All-purpose liquid fertilizer
diluted half strength*
※
Light
*4 to 6 hours, or more, direct morning
or afternoon sun*
※
Watering Schedule
*Every 1 to 2 weeks from March
through September, every 2 to 3 weeks
from October through February,
more often in hot weather*
※
Fertilizing Schedule
*Once a month from March
through August*
※
Hardiness
To 40°F
※
When Blooms Appear
Spring to summer
※

ECHINOCACTUS GRUSONII, GOLDEN BARREL CACTUS

Perhaps best described as bowling balls designed by a surrealist, this species of barrel cactus has stunning golden spines on a green globelike shape. There is, however, another, rather unkind name for this plant: mother-in-law's armchair. ¶ The golden barrel cactus is slow growing—a ten-year-old plant might reach only 6 inches high—and long-lived. Buy the size you would like to enjoy, for it may take years for a plant in a 4-inch container to reach an impressive girth. In its native habitat, a specimen grows 36 to 39 inches wide and, as an adult, blooms with yellow flowers that have pointed petals. The smaller plants do not bloom, but the straw yellow thickly growing spines give the cactus such a glowing aura that gardeners delight in the spectacle of the plant alone. ¶ If you choose to overwinter the plant indoors—it makes an attractive addition to your indoor containers—keep the plant on the dry side and in a cool, 50°F location. **¶ HOW TO DO IT ¶** Place the plant outside in an area with direct sunlight for 4 to 6 hours, or more, each day. In the growing season, from March through September, water every one to two weeks. In fall and winter, from October through February, water every two to three weeks. Move the plant to a protected location when the temperature drops below 45°F. Fertilize, after you water, once a month from March through August with an all-purpose liquid fertilizer diluted half strength and applied according to the directions on the container.

Golden Barrel Cactus
Echinocactus grusonii

What You Need
All-purpose liquid fertilizer
diluted half strength

Light
4 to 6 hours, or more, direct morning
or afternoon sun

Watering Schedule
Every 1 to 2 weeks from March
through September, every 2 to 3 weeks
from October through February,
water more often in hot weather

Fertilizing Schedule
Once a month from March
through August

Hardiness
To 45°F

When Blooms Appear
When the plant is over 15 inches
in diameter

ECHEVERIA IMBRICATA, HEN-AND-CHICKS

Hen-and-chicks, the old-fashioned succulent often seen in older gardens as tight border plants, shines on its own when potted in a container. With just a few plants centered in the pot, the attractive rosette design and cool color of the leaves makes a knockout container for a special spot. Pairing succulents with perennials adds texture and visual interest. The celadon green-gray of the succulent hen-and-chicks goes well with the fuzzy gray leaves of the perennial lamb's-ears (Stachys byzantina). Both plants are quite drought resistant, so they do well in pots watered every couple of weeks throughout the summer. You can train lamb's-ears to drape over the sides or pinch them back for a gentle fringe around the container. As the hen-and-chicks grow, pinch back the little offshoots to maintain a tidy look. Match the sea green palette of the plants with a pale green pot for the maximum effect. ¶ **HOW TO DO IT** ¶ Before planting, submerge the plants in their containers in a sink or bucket of water until air bubbles cease to appear. Fill the container with potting mix to within 2 inches of the rim. Water the mix until it is thoroughly moist. Scoop out holes large enough for the roots of the plants. Gently remove each plant and its potting mix from its container and plant it so that the top of the root ball is level with the surface of the mix. Arrange the hen-and-chicks in the center and the lamb's-ears evenly around the rim of the container. Fill the holes with mix, packing it gently around the roots. Pat down the surface and water to fill in any air pockets. Mulch plants with organic compost spread 1 inch deep. ¶ Place outside in an area with direct sunlight for four to six hours, or more, each day. In the growing season, from March through September, water every one to two weeks. In fall and winter, from October through February, water every two to three weeks. Move the plant to a protected location when the temperature drops below 40°F. Fertilize, after you water, once a month from March through August with an all-purpose liquid fertilizer diluted half strength and applied according to the directions on the container.

Hen-and-Chicks
Echeveria byzantina
Lamb's-Ears
Stachys byzantina
❧

What You Need
3 rosettes of Echeveria imbricata
6-pack or 6 rooted cuttings of
Stachys byzantina
1 container 9 inches in diameter
and 10 inches deep
Fast-draining potting mix
such as cactus mix
All-purpose liquid fertilizer
diluted half strength
❧

Light
4 to 6 hours, or more, direct sun
❧

Watering Schedule
Every 1 to 2 weeks from March
through September, every 2 to 3 weeks
from October to February,
more often in hot weather
❧

Fertilizing Schedule
Once a month from March through August
❧

Hardiness
To 40°F
❧

When Blooms Appear
Spring to summer
❧

CHAMAECEREUS SILVESTRII, PEANUT CACTUS

This small cactus rewards the gardener with rapid growth—in cactus terms, of course. The common name comes from the appearance of freely produced pups, which resemble peanuts, complete with the pebbly textured shell, but with the addition of spines. ¶ In spring and summer, the cactus is covered with exotic, fire-engine red blooms shaped like vases and almost 3 inches long. The peanut cactus is popular with hybridizers, and some hybrids can be ordered from mail-order catalogues. Since the offsets drop off at the touch and propagate so easily, find someone who has a plant so you can take home several pups. Even the smallest ones often produce a bloom. ¶ Grow this cactus in a shallow pot that allows it room to expand horizontally. Make sure to decrease watering in fall and winter even though the plant looks shriveled. Begin to water gradually and fertilize again when the weather warms up. For the best production of blooms, keep the plant cool and dry in winter, but never below 35°F. Begin to water lavishly only when buds appear. Too much water too early encourages the plant to grow rather than to bloom. ¶ **HOW TO DO IT** ¶ Place the plant outside in an area with direct sunlight for four to six hours, or more, each day. In the growing season, from March through September, water every one to two weeks. In the fall and winter, from October through February, water every two to three weeks. Fertilize, after you water, once a month from March through August with an all-purpose liquid fertilizer diluted half strength and applied according to the directions on the container. Move the plant to a protected overhang or inside when the temperature drops down below 35°F.

Peanut Cactus
Chamaecereus silvestrii

What You Need
All-purpose liquid plant fertilizer diluted half strength

Light
3 to 4 hours, or more, direct morning or afternoon sun

Watering Schedule
Every 1 to 2 weeks from March through September, every 2 to 3 weeks from October through February, more often in hot weather

Fertilizing Schedule
Once a month from March through August

Hardiness
To 35°F

When Blooms Appear
Spring through early summer

IN A SMALL
PATCH
OF LAND

R egardless of where you live and the range of winter to summer temperatures, there are cacti and succulents to ornament your garden and provide color, texture, and flower bloom from spring to fall. For rock walls or areas of the garden beyond irrigation lines, these plants are hardy enough to go for weeks without watering. Whether you need a low-growing ground cover like an Echeveria or a tall stately bedding plant like Sedum spectabile, or even a hedge of Opuntia, there is a plant to fill almost every gardening situation. ❧ For gardeners planting low-water, low-maintenance gardens in mild-winter areas, interspersing cacti and succulents among drought-resistant perennials makes a water-wise garden. Succulents can edge beds, perform as ground covers, or add color and texture as vertical accents or display planting. Just make sure to match the watering requirements of perennials with those of the succulents and cacti you add to the beds. Gardeners in freeze areas can always mix the hardy with the frost sensitive by lifting the tender plants in the fall and overwintering them in containers inside. ❧ Some succulents and cacti endure freezing temperatures with the ease of penguins and polar bears. Marginal varieties make it through with a bit of protection, whether a southern exposure with an overhang, a covering of mulch, or a portable greenhouse extension. Local nurseries and horticulturists can help you choose the best varieties for your climate.

ALOE SAPONARIA

Although some aloes grow to the size of trees, 18 feet or so, this plant takes little space, requires minimal water, and adds color to the garden for most of the early summer. Speckled and splashed with dashes of white, the sawtooth-edged leaves grow about 8 to 10 inches long in tidy rosettes. One or two of these succulents gradually multiply to fill a larger space, so plan to set out about one plant per square foot. Because these aloes tenaciously cling to hillsides and perform well in quick-draining soil, they can provide some erosion control. Equally important, they bring a lively texture to a sloping piece of land without the need for irrigation. The tall bloom stalks appear in spring and last through early summer. The salmon pink flowers in clusters make long-lasting additions to flower arrangements. ¶ If the plants grow too close together, spoiling the symmetry of their form, divide them in the late summer by cutting the connecting stem and separating the plants. Extras can be tucked into low-water garden beds or planted in containers. Gardeners in frost-prone areas can grow the plants in containers and protect them in the winter. ¶ **HOW TO DO IT** ¶ Before planting, submerge the plants in their containers in a sink or bucket of water until air bubbles cease to appear. Make sure to prepare the soil properly (see page 34). Water the planting area until the soil is thoroughly moist. Scoop out holes large enough for the roots of the plants. Add 1 teaspoon pelleted, slow-release, low-nitrogen fertilizer to the bottom of each hole. Gently remove each plant and its potting mix from its container and plant it so that the top of the root ball is level with the surface of the soil. Fill the hole with soil, packing it gently around the roots. Pat down the surface and water to fill in any air pockets. Mulch plants with organic compost spread 2 inches deep. ¶ Until the plants become established

Aloe saponaria

What You Need
4 plants
4 square feet of prepared ground
Pelleted, slow-release, low-nitrogen fertilizer
Organic compost

Light
4 hours or more direct sun

Watering Schedule
New plants every 2 weeks, established plants once a month from March through September, every 6 weeks from October through February, more often in hot weather

Fertilizing Schedule
Once in fall or early spring

Hardiness
To 32°F

When Blooms Appear
Late spring through early summer

and show new growth, water them every two weeks. In the growing season, March through September, water once a month. In fall and winter, from October through February, water every six weeks. In hot weather, you may need to increase watering. Fertilize once in fall or early spring by working a pelleted, slow-release, low-nitrogen fertilizer lightly into the soil around the base of the plant according to the directions on the container.

OPUNTIA BURBANKII, BURBANK'S SPINELESS CACTUS

Luther Burbank—some say a crank, others a mad genius, still others a brilliant plant breeder—was convinced that a spineless cactus grown as food for foraging cattle could be useful for otherwise unproductive arid areas. From 1907 to 1925, he imported many varieties of Opuntia in his attempts to hybridize a pad without spines. In his test gardens next to his house in the temperate climate of Santa Rosa, California, now a public garden and historical site, you can see his final success. A huge spineless cactus dating from 1925 luxuriously spreads out along the old carriage house. ¶ If you want a cactus next to a path or as a garden hedge this cactus grows almost as large as the prickly pear—6 feet high and 8 feet across—but without the hazardous spines. Large 12-inch pads in sea foam green make a handsome addition to any garden as well as an edible vegetable for kitchen use. Very frost tolerant, it survives temperatures down to 20°F. The large yellow flowers that appear in summer are followed by edible fruit. This variety is available in many nurseries and is also listed in mail-order catalogues. Should you be unable to locate one, you can substitute Opuntia compressa, an almost identical variety with a few spines along the edge of the pads that fall off. ¶ **HOW TO DO IT** ¶ Before planting, submerge the plant in its containers in a sink or bucket of water until air bubbles cease to appear. Make sure to prepare the soil properly (see page 34). Water the planting area until the soil is thoroughly moist. Scoop out a hole large enough for the roots of the plant. Add 1 teaspoon pelleted, slow-release, low-nitrogen fertilizer to the bottom of the hole. Gently remove the plant and its potting mix from its container and plant it so that the top of the root ball is level with the surface of the soil. Fill the hole with soil, packing it gently around the roots. Pat down the surface and water to fill in any air pockets. Mulch the plant with organic compost spread 2 inches deep. ¶ Until the plant

Burbank's Spineless Cactus
Opuntia burbankii

What You Need
1 plant
4 square feet of prepared ground
Pelleted, slow-release, low-nitrogen fertilizer
Organic compost
❧
Light
4 hours or more direct sun
❧
Watering Schedule
New plant every 2 weeks, established plant once a month from March through September, every 6 weeks from October through February, more often in hot weather
❧
Fertilizing Schedule
Once in fall or early spring
❧
Hardiness
To 20°F
❧
When Blooms Appear
Late spring to summer
❧

becomes established and shows new growth, water it every two weeks. In the growing season, March through September, water once a month. In fall and winter, from October through February, water every six weeks. In hot weather, you may need to increase watering. Fertilize once in fall or early spring by working a pelleted, slow-release, low-nitrogen fertilizer lightly into the soil around the base of the plant according to the directions on the container.

OPUNTIA FICUS-INDICA, PRICKLY PEAR

These plants are ubiquitous around older homes in the West and Southwest. Beloved by gardeners and gourmets for their blooms, pads, and fruit, they thrive on neglect, growing larger and larger often with almost no summer water. As their pads drop off and root, they spread to make dense prickly walls or vast patches. If they are suited to their planting spot, they can grow to 15 feet tall and 5 or 6 feet wide, or more, so make sure to plan space for them. The 4-inch blooms are bright yellow, and the ripening round red or yellow tunas, or fruit, so decorate the plant that if you squint, you might think you have a summertime Christmas tree. Use some care when harvesting the fruits, for they, too, have spines. ¶ Prickly pear can withstand an amount of cold weather and even some freezing temperatures but, unlike its relatives, will not survive snowy winters. In climates where winter temperatures hover just above freezing, try planting it along a protected south-facing wall. ¶ **HOW TO DO IT** ¶ Before planting, submerge the plant in its container in a sink or bucket of water until air bubbles cease to appear. Make sure to prepare the soil properly (see page 34). Water the planting area until the soil is thoroughly moist. Scoop out a hole large enough for the roots of the plant. Add 1 teaspoon pelleted, slow-release, low-nitrogen fertilizer to the bottom of the hole. Gently remove the plant and its potting mix from its container and plant it so that the top of the root ball is level with the surface of the soil. Fill the hole with soil, packing it gently around the roots. Pat down the surface and water to fill in any air pockets. Mulch the plant with organic compost spread 2 inches deep. ¶ Until the plant becomes established and shows new growth, water it every two weeks. In the growing season, March through September, water once a month. In fall and winter, from October through February, water every six weeks. In hot weather, you may need to increase watering.

Prickly Pear
Opuntia ficus-indica

❧

What You Need
1 plant
4 square feet of prepared ground
Pelleted, slow-release, low-nitrogen fertilizer
Organic compost

❧

Light
4 hours or more of direct sun

❧

Watering Schedule
New plant every 2 weeks, established plant once a month from March through September, every 6 weeks from October through February

❧

Fertilizing Schedule
Once in fall or early spring

❧

Hardiness
To 32°F

❧

When Blooms Appear
Late spring to summer

❧

Fertilize once in fall or early spring by working a pelleted, slow-release, low-nitrogen fertilizer lightly into the soil around the base of the plant according to the directions on the container.

A ROCK WALL GARDEN

Making a rock garden, in part of a wall, along steps, or as a mound, creates a landscape ornament and increases garden space when room in beds or containers is limited. Walls or mounds can be built with large rocks or rubble. Many a gardener has spied crews breaking up sidewalks and returned in a car to haul away the fragments. Handsome low walls edging raised beds, retaining walls, or mounds can be constructed by offsetting slabs or rocks to create nooks and crannies filled with equal parts of soil and cactus mix. ¶ Consider color and texture when designing the location of the plants. If you choose to work with the green-gray rosettes of Echeveria, then combine with the same shades of Sempervivum, also a low-growing rosette. Create a contrast with the creeping leaves of green, pink, and white, Sedum spurium 'Tricolor,' mixed with Sempervivum hybrids whose leaves carry green tones but have an edge color of bright red. Mix small-leaved plants like Sedum and Crassula with larger ones for contrast. ¶ If you live in a cold climate, limit your garden to hardy Sempervivum, for they survive low temperatures and come in an wide variety of colors. It is easy to accent your planting with some of the more exotic succulents, which you can lift to winter inside in containers, then set outside again in the spring. ¶ **HOW TO DO IT** ¶ Before planting, submerge the plants in their containers in a sink or bucket of water until air bubbles cease to appear. Fill the planting nooks with equal parts of cactus potting mix and soil. Water the mix until it is thoroughly moist. Scoop out holes large enough for the roots of the plants. Add 1 teaspoon pelleted, slow-release, low-nitrogen fertilizer to the bottom of each hole. Gently remove each plant and its potting mix from its container and plant it so that the top of the root ball is level with the surface of the soil. Fill the holes with soil and mix, packing gently around the roots. Pat down the surface and water to fill in any air pockets. Mulch ✐

Assorted low-growing succulents
Crassula anomala
Echeveria elegans, 'Lola,'
E. agavoides, E. secunda,
Sedum spurium 'Tricolor', S. lydium,
S. hirtum, S. spathulifolium,
Sempervivum tectorum,
S. montanum, S. giuseppii

❧

What You Need
24 plants in 6-packs
4 square feet of rock wall,
or mounded rock garden
Cactus potting mix
Pelleted, slow-release, low-nitrogen fertilizer
Organic compost

❧

Light
4 hours or more direct sun

❧

Watering Schedule
New plants every 2 weeks, established
plants once a month from March through
September, every 6 weeks from October
through February, more often in hot weather

❧

Fertilizing Schedule
Once in fall or early spring

❧

Hardiness
To 45°F

❧

When Blooms Appear
Spring and summer depending upon variety

❧

the plants with organic compost. ¶ Until the plants become established and show new growth, water them every two weeks. In the growing season, March through September, water once a month. In fall and winter, from October through February, water every six weeks. In hot weather, you may need to increase watering. Fertilize once in fall or early spring by working a pelleted, slow-release, low-nitrogen fertilizer lightly into the soil around the base of the plants according to the directions on the container.

Sempervivum, Houseleek

The Latin name of this genus means "ever living." Indeed, these small—no more than 6 inches across and 2 inches high—plants are hardy enough to survive in cold winter areas. Not even snow and sleet bother them. The most common type, S. tectorum, has been grown in Europe for centuries, the tenacious roots securing the soil on sod roofs. In fact, the species name, tectorum, means "roofs." Sometimes these plants are called by or sold under the common name of hen-and-chicks, so be careful not to confuse them with Echeveria, which goes by the same name. ¶ The many species of Sempervivum vary in height and color. Once you have seen them, you will recognize the similarity of their tight rosettes. After the rosettes set seed, the main stems die, but they throw off so many offsets that the border or bed in which they are planted stays full. ¶ The countless hybrids range in appearance from fuzzy to smooth and shiny, from variegated to solid colored. In some varieties, the tips of the leaves look as if they have been dipped in burgundy paint. Because Sempervivum grow in tight clusters, they are often used as border plants. For a contrast, pair them with bright, low-growing annuals like deep-red miniature zinnias or burgundy pompom dahlias. Low-growing Sedum make a handsome ground cover underneath the Sempervivum. ¶ **HOW TO DO IT** ¶ Before planting, submerge the plants in their containers in a sink or bucket of water until air bubbles cease to appear. Make sure to prepare the soil properly (see page 34). Water the planting area until the soil is thoroughly moist. Scoop out holes large enough for the roots of the plants. Add ¹/₂ teaspoon pelleted, slow-release, low-nitrogen fertilizer to the bottom of each hole. Gently remove each plant and its potting mix from its container and plant it so that the top of the root ball is level with the surface of the soil. Fill the hole with soil, packing it gently around the roots. Pat down the surface and water to fill in any air pockets. Mulch the plants ✒

Houseleek
Assorted Sempervivum, such as
S. tectorum, S. 'Commander Hay',
S. grandiflorum, and S. montanum

What You Need
4 plants
4 square feet of prepared ground
Pelleted, slow-release, low-nitrogen fertilizer
Organic compost

Light
4 hours or more direct sun

Watering Schedule
New plants every 2 weeks, established plants once a month from March through September, every 6 weeks from October through February

Fertilizing Schedule
Once in fall or early spring

Hardiness
Some types to 32°F, others to 0°F

When Blooms Appear
Late spring to summer
🦎

with organic compost spread 2 inches deep. ¶ Until the plants become established and show new growth, water them every two weeks. In the growing season, March through September, water once a month. In fall and winter, from October through February, water every six weeks. In hot weather, you may need to increase watering. Fertilize once in fall or early spring by working a pelleted, slow-release, low-nitrogen fertilizer lightly into the soil around the base of the plants according to the directions on the container.

A DROUGHT-RESISTANT GARDEN

Much research has taken place in the last ten years to design gardens that sip water in a miserly fashion while still providing rich vistas of colored foliage in a mixture of textures. As you can imagine, succulents and cacti feature prominently along with grasses and drought-tolerant perennials to create landscapes that please the eye and scrimp on water usage. ¶ *Mixing cacti and succulents into perennial beds takes planning. Use low-growing succulents toward the front of a bed, or mix aloes with a lively low-growing ground cover. Work in the sedums along pathways, around rocks, or underneath cacti. Experiment with blending leaf textures and colors, the rounded leaves of succulents with the finely drawn grasses and herbs. Use variegated green-and-white grasses with light-toned or two-toned succulents.* ¶ **HOW TO DO IT** ¶ Before planting, submerge the plants in their containers in a sink or bucket of water until air bubbles cease to appear. Make sure to prepare the soil properly (see page 34). Water the planting area until the soil is thoroughly moist. Scoop out holes large enough for the roots of the plants. Add 1 teaspoon pelleted, slow-release, low-nitrogen fertilizer to the bottom of each hole. Gently remove each plant and its potting mix from its container and plant it so that the top of the root ball is level with the surface of the soil. Fill the hole with soil, packing it gently around the roots. Pat down the surface and water to fill in any air pockets. Mulch the plants with organic compost spread 2 inches deep. ¶ Until the plants becomes established and show new growth, water them every two weeks. In the growing season, March through September, water once a month. In fall and winter, from October through February, water every six weeks. In hot weather, you may need to increase watering. Fertilize once in fall or early spring by working a pelleted, slow-release, low-nitrogen fertilizer lightly into the soil around the base of the plants according to the directions on the container.

Assortment of cacti and succulents, grasses, and drought-resistant perennials

❧

What You Need
Pelleted, slow-release, low-nitrogen fertilizer
Organic compost

❧

Light
4 hours or more of direct sun

❧

Watering Schedule
New plants every 2 weeks, established plants once a month from March through September, every 6 weeks from October through February

❧

Fertilizing Schedule
Once in fall or early spring

❧

Hardiness
To 32°F

❧

When Blooms Appear
Late spring to summer

❧

Exotic

cacti and

succulents

To many gardeners, cacti and succulents seem quite exotic. The selections in this chapter, however, have some of the most exquisite flowers and the most unusual forms. They also

offer a growing adventure for the gardener. These plants may be a bit difficult to locate in local nurseries. The mail-order sources on the resource list (see page 105) should help you locate a supplier. ❧ Consider the requirements of these plants in relation to your climate and the environment of your home before you purchase them to make sure that you can provide the light and temperature they need. Be prepared to check them regularly and follow any specific regimes they require to reward you with sustained growth and bloom. They may be a bit more unforgiving of erratic watering or inadequate light. Make sure to move those plants accustomed to tropical temperatures away from windows in winter, lest the chill seeping through the glass drops indoor temperatures too low. Your reward in bursts of extravagant bloom and elegant growth goes hand in hand with your satisfaction in your stewardship of these most unusual of the earth's greenery.

Pilosocereus glaucescens multiflorus, Brazilian Blue Cactus

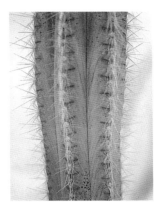

One look at this glorious slate-blue cactus, and the collector's heart turns over. Few cacti have this wonderful rock-cool color. These plants were once very rare, but now can be purchased from specialty nurseries and mail-order sources. In their native Brazil, these cacti grow to the size of a small tree and in summer are covered with white flowers. Grown indoors in containers, they slowly edge upright to 4 to 5 feet and develop branches, but rarely flower. These plants prefer a warm environment and should be protected from temperatures below 50°F. You should be able to locate three varieties showing off their blueness, all with the same cultivation needs. ¶ **HOW TO DO IT** ¶

Place the plant indoors in an area with direct sunlight for four to six hours, or more, each day. In the growing season, from March through September, water every one to two weeks. In fall and winter, from October through February, water every two to three weeks. In winter, keep the plant in a warm room above 68°F, and in summer, place outdoors in filtered sunlight. Fertilize, after you water, once a month from March through August with an all-purpose liquid fertilizer diluted half strength and applied according to the directions on the container.

Brazilian Blue Cactus
Pilosocereus glaucescens
var. multiflorus, P. azureus,
P. pachycladus

What You Need
*All-purpose liquid fertilizer
diluted half strength*

Light
*4 to 6 hours, or more, direct morning or
afternoon sun indoors, filtered sun outdoors*

Watering Schedule
*Every 1 to 2 weeks from March
through September, every 2 to 3 weeks
from October through February,
more often in hot weather*

Fertilizing Schedule
*Once a month from March
through August*

Hardiness
To 50°F

When Blooms Appear
Not in cultivation

DIOSCOREA ELEPHANTIPES, ELEPHANT'S-FOOT

Most of the year, this curious member of the succulent family mimics an age-whitened and cracked piece of wood. Then, in spring, it sprouts a viny stem of leaves that can creep out 10 feet or more. In the summer, small white flowers tinged with green appear in clusters along the twining stem. ¶ What appears to be the block of wood is actually a tuber. The Dioscorea genus, with some five hundred species, includes the edible yam. The leaves of Elephant's-foot resemble those of yam plants. The elephant's-foot is also called hottentot bread after the Hottentots, the South African Bushmen and Bantus, who ate the tuber in times of extreme famine, something you would not want to try. ¶ Unlike other succulents, this plant grows in winter and is dormant in summer, so water sparingly over the summer, about every 6 weeks. Place the plant in a warm, 68°F room throughout the winter months, and when you see the green shoot sprout, usually in December, then begin to water regularly. ¶ **HOW TO DO IT** ¶ Place the plant indoors in an area with at least four hours of direct sunlight each day. Water lightly every two weeks after the sprout emerges through May, and every two months from June through December. In winter, keep the plant in a warm room above 68°F. Fertilize, after you water, once a month from December through May with an all-purpose liquid fertilizer diluted half strength and applied according to the directions on the container.

Elephant's-Foot
Dioscorea elephantipes
or Mexican Elephant's Foot
D. macrostachya

What You Need
*All-purpose liquid fertilizer
diluted half strength*

Light
4 hours direct morning or afternoon sun

Watering Schedule
*Every 2 weeks after sprout emerges,
usually December through May, every 2
months from June through December*

Fertilizing Schedule
*Once a month from December
through May*

Hardiness
To 50°F

When Blooms Appear
Late spring

CONSOLEA RUBESCENS

With its bright patent-leather green skin dotted with glochids, this cactus looks like no other. When it is immature, its flat limbs and green color make it look like a familiar cartoon character, hence its nickname, not really an official common name, of Gumbee. As the plant matures beyond 2 or 3 feet, the joints become rounder, like those of other cacti. The gumbee cactus has white areoles but no spines to speak of, making it a safe plant in households with children. As a container plant, it rarely blooms, but when it does, yellow flowers form in late spring. It grows quite fast, for cactus, but let it stay a bit cramped in its container for several years before repotting.

¶ **HOW TO DO IT** ¶ Place the plant indoors in an area with at least four hours of direct sun each day. In the growing season, from March through September, water every one to two weeks. In fall and winter, from October through February, water every two to three weeks. In hot weather, you may need to increase watering. Fertilize, after you water, once a month from March through August with an all-purpose liquid fertilizer diluted half strength and applied according to the container.

Consolea rubescens
❧

What You Need
*All-purpose liquid fertilizer
diluted half strength*
❧

Light
4 hours direct morning or afternoon sun
❧

Watering Schedule
*Every 1 to 2 weeks from March
through September, every 2 to 3 weeks
from October through February,
more often in hot weather*
❧

Fertilizing Schedule
*Once a month from March
through August*
❧

Hardiness
To 40°F
❧

When Blooms Appear
Not in cultivation
❧

EUPHORBIA TIRUCALLI, PENCIL TREE

The smooth, leafless branches of this succulent give the plant its common name. With new growth, small leaves sprout but quickly fall off the plant, leaving a stark silhouette that makes a dramatic showing backlit against a plain-colored wall. ¶ Milkbrush, another name, refers to the milky sap that oozes from the plant when a branch is broken. The white sap is a strong irritant, so make sure to wash off any that gets on your skin. Always a good rule with any plant, but doubly important with *Euphorbia*, make sure to keep children and pets from playing with or nibbling on any of its branches. ¶ Although the plant grows to 30 feet in its native habitat in South Africa, it can easily be maintained in a pot. Under suitable conditions and with time, a container plant can grow to be 6 to 8 feet tall. You can lightly prune it by cutting off branches that intersect or cross through the center to shape the plant and keep it from becoming too much of a tangle. These clippings, potted in cactus potting mix, sprout to make new plants (see pages 38–39). ¶ **HOW TO DO IT** ¶ Place the plant indoors in an area with bright light but no direct sunlight. In the growing season, from March through September, water every one to two weeks. In the late fall and winter, from October through February, water every two to three weeks. In hot weather, you may need to increase watering. Fertilize, after you water, once a month from March through August with an all-purpose liquid fertilizer diluted half strength and applied according to the directions on the container.

Pencil Tree
Euphorbia tirucalli

What You Need
*All-purpose liquid fertilizer
diluted half strength*

Light
Bright light without direct sun

Watering Schedule
*Every 1 to 2 weeks from March
through September, every 2 to 3 weeks
from October through February,
more often in hot weather*

Fertilizing Schedule
*Once a month from March
through August*

Hardiness
To 45°F

When Blooms Appear
Insignificant flowers

Mail-order sources

Sources

Abbey Garden Cacti and Succulents
P.O. Box 2249
La Habra, CA 90632
(310) 905-3520

Great Petaluma Desert
5010 Bodega Avenue
Petaluma, CA 94952
(707) 778-8278

Grigsby Cactus Gardens
2326 Bella Vista Drive
Vista, CA 92084
(619) 727-1323

Henrietta's Nursery
1345 Brawley
Fresno, CA 93711
(209) 275-2166

Highland Succulents
1446 Bear Run Road
Gallipolis, OH 45631
(614) 256-1428

Loehman's Cactus Patch
P.O. Box 871
Paramount, CA 90723
(310) 428-4501

Logee's Greenhouses
141 North Street
Dept. AH
Danielson, CT 06239
(203) 774-8038

Los Angeles Plant Co.
856 Mason Road
Vista, CA 92084
(619) 726-7789

Mile's to Go
P.O. Box 6
Cortaro, AZ 85652
Write for information

Northridge Gardens
9821 White Oak Avenue
Northridge, CA 91325
(818) 349-9797

Oasis
Cactus & Succulents
84 London Way
Sonoma, CA 95476
(707) 996-8732

Rare Plant Research
132345 Southeast Harold
Portland, OR 97236
Write for information

Valley Cactus
Route 2, Box 318C
Adel, GA 31620
(912) 896-7319

BIBLIOGRAPHY

FOR MORE INFORMATION ON CACTI AND SUCCULENTS ALSO CONTACT:

Amateur's Digest
Marina Welham, Editor
8591 Lochside Drive
Sidney, BC V8L 1M5
Canada
$20 per year for 6 issues of an informative journal

Cactus and Succulent Society
for general information:
Dr. Seymour Linden
1535 Reeves Street
Los Angeles, CA 90035
(310) 556-1923
Fax (310) 286-9629

for membership information:
Melinda Fusaro
P.O. Box 35034
Des Moines, IO 50315-0301
$30 per year for 6 journals and 6 newsletters

Andersohn, Gunter.
Cacti and Succulents.
Wakefield, England: EP Publishing
Limited, 1983.

Becherer, Franz.
Success with Cacti.
London: Merehurst, 1993.

Borg, John.
*Cacti: A Gardener's Handbook for Their
Identification and Cultivation.*
London: Blandford Press, 1973.

Hortus Third Dictionary.
New York: Macmillan, 1976.

Kramer, Jack.
Cacti and Other Succulents.
New York: Harry N. Abrams, Inc.,
Publishers, 1977.

Martin, Margaret J., P. R. Chapman,
and H. A. Auger.
Cacti and Their Cultivation.
New York: Winchester Press, 1971.

Quiros, Alice, and Barbara L. Young.
*The World of Cactus and Succulents and Other
Water-Thrifty Plants.*
San Ramon, California: Ortho Books,
1977.

Index

ACKNOWLEDGMENTS

A book comes to life with as many people helping as there are thorns on a *melocactus*. Mickey Choate, Carolyn Larson, and Susan Lescher of The Lescher Agency began the process, much like planting seeds. Kermit and Shirley Puls of Oasis, Jerry Wright of Great Petaluma Desert, Vince and Clare Amendola, Linn Briner, David Feix, and Ray Mishler added with advice and information, as generous as a desert rain. Dick Turner and the Ruth Bancroft Garden extended a gracious invitation to allow us to photograph in their glorious garden, as did the Huntington Botanical Garden in Pasadena. Thanks Susan and Molly; Madame Lisa and Slim; Wolfgang and Inga at the Red Desert, San Francisco, California; Alta at the Gardener, Berkeley, California; and Dorrit, Leslie and Mitch, Daphne, and Joan. The staff of Chronicle Books—Leslie Jonath, Sarah Putman, and Amy Torack—helped keep us going. Like choosing the right container, Aufuldish and Warinner put everything together in their stylish mode. As ever to our families Bruce Le Favour and Daniel and Arann Harris, who, like an oasis on the desert, provide us with the sweet water and sumptuous fruits after hard work.